Linda Parker

Vegetarian Breakfast Cookbook

Simple, Delicious and Healthy Vegetarian Breakfast Recipes

Table of Contents

Introduction

Breakfasts have always been of prime importance in most families. If your family is one that doesn't stress on eating a wholesome breakfast, then it is about time it does!

When you split the word 'Breakfast' into 'Break' and 'Fast' you will truly understand the meaning behind it all. The reason this meal is one of the most important meals of the day is because it *breaks a fast* of not eating anything through the night, for the entire duration of your night sleep. So when you wake up, you need to eat soon because this is the meal that gets you geared up and started.

All the more important however, is the rise in the trend of adopting vegetarianism as a meal choice across the globe. Why are people adopting to this so much these days?

- It is great for the environment. Vegetarianism reduces carbon footprint and is, in fact, a way of giving back to your very own planet.
- Whatever said and done, it is most definitely the healthier option. A vegetarian diet keeps the heart going strong and the body doing well.
- For those animal lovers out there, there is no other option really. To protect animals of all sorts, animal-loving vegetarians will do what helps the animals of this planet the best- that is not including animal meat in their diets.

There is no denying that a vegetarian diet can at sometimes get quite boring and monotonous. Given the rising popularity of this diet today, there are several options available for you to follow. This book throws light on the various vegetarian breakfast options that you can follow, which will make you love your diet all the more!

Chapter 1: Basics of Vegetarian Eating

There is a huge group of people around the world that are big on the aspect of vegetarian diets and follow it very seriously. You have probably come across people who talk about eliminating red meat from their diets completely and eat only chicken or fish and thus consider themselves vegetarians. Looking at that example, there are indeed several types of vegetarians- lacto ovo vegetarians are those who eat eggs and dairy and no other meat, chicken or fish apart from the certified vegetarian food. Lacto Vegetarians are those who exclude dairy products from their diet and include plant based foods. Then you have your vegans who are your true vegetarians, thus eating only plants based foods and no animal flesh whatsoever, no dairy products and no eggs. Then you also have the raw foodists who don't heat up their food above a temperature of 118 degrees and fruitarians who have a simple diet consisting of just fruits and foods that are considered fruits such as tomatoes, avocados and bell peppers.

However, a well planned for vegetarian diet is one of the best and healthiest ways of meeting your dietary requirements and also fulfilling your nutritional needs. In order to create the foundation of a healthy vegetarian diet, you need to understand the basis of it all and the ideology on which it stands. Bringing in variety into your diet is one of the key factors to sustaining it for a longer period of time.

One of the most important things to ensure while going on all vegetarian diet is to ensure that your fill of nutrients such as proteins, enzymes and calcium are covered.

Calcium intake is ensured by adding green vegetables to your diet such as kale, collard greens, spinach and broccoli. Foods rich in calcium also include fresh fruit juices, milk, soy milk and yogurt and tofu or paneer.

Iron is another crucial component that is present in the red blood cells and constantly needs to be kept under check. Peas, beans, lentils, grains and leafy green vegetables are all considered reliable sources of iron. As most vegetarians strictly follow an all plant produce iron is not as easily absorbed into the body, thus you need to work a lot harder and eat better food in order to gain the required amount of calcium. Strawberries, cabbage, broccoli, tomatoes or any other fruit variety are most helpful in doing the same.

Vegetarians that consume fish in small portions are covered when it comes to adequate intake of omega-3 fatty acids since they are one of the best sources for that. However, other vegetarians can consume handfuls of walnuts, flaxseed or flaxseed powder, soybeans, and cook in canola or soy oil to ensure the same.

Protein is brought to the table from foods such as eggs, milk and milk products, legumes, seeds, nuts, lentils and grains for all vegetarians. While a lean cut of meat will also do the trick, it is not necessary for one to turn non-vegetarian to get their fill of proteins.

Your vitamin intake such as vitamin D, B-12 and C must also be given special attention. Intake of Vitamin D gives special attention to bone health and is found in foods such as soy, rice, milk and some cereals. Adequate sun exposure every day is suggested for parents and kinds alike. A lack of vitamin B-12 is normally noticed in people following a vegan diet. Thus it is important to take vitamin supplements, vitamin B-12 filled products and even products rich in soy. This to some extent will cover the lack of the vitamin.

A vegetarian diet is said to be one that focuses solely on an array of plants as the base of its food. This can include anything from all types of vegetables to fruits to dried beans, grains, nuts and even seeds. Due to a large variety of recipes that can be cooked up with these ingredients, a vegetarian definitely does have enough and more variety that he can create for himself through his lifetime.

Chapter 2: Top 20 Breakfast Recipes

Breakfast Casserole

This breakfast just makes you want to take holiday from work and routine life because it is scrumptious twist to your regular oatmeal.

Serves 2
Ingredients:
For the oatmeal:

- ½ cup regular oats
- 2 cups soy milk
- 1 banana, large
- 1 tbsp. chia seeds, optional
- 1 sweet potato, small, peeled and chopped
- 2 tsp. vanilla extract
- Pinch of ground cinnamon and nutmeg
- 2 tbsp. maple syrup

For the topping:

- 1/3 cup chopped pecans
- 2 tbsp. flour
- ¼ cup brown sugar
- 2 tbsp. of butter

Directions:

- Start by preheating the oven to 350F. Add water and sweet potato to a dish and bring to boil. Once done, drain out the water and keep it aside
- Move on to cooking the oats with milk and chia seeds. In the meanwhile, mash the sweet potato with the banana, using a potato masher. Add the cinnamon mixture and maple syrup to it and check for seasoning as required.
- Proceed to making the topping by mixing the pecans, butter, flour and brown sugar together. Put the oatmeal into a casserole dish and spread it out evenly. Now add the topping on the oatmeal.
- Bake for 20 minutes and broil for about 5-7 minutes to make the topping brown and crunchy.

Gingerbread and Pumpkin Smoothie

This is yet another easy breakfast recipe that you can have on the go. It is a low fat and low carb breakfast option.

Serves 1
Ingredients:

- 1 cup of almond milk
- ¼ cup of rolled oats
- ½ cup of pureed pumpkin
- 1 tbsp. of chia seeds
- 1 small fresh banana
- 1 teaspoon of ground cinnamon
- 1 teaspoon of ginger
- A pinch of nutmeg

Directions:

- Soak the chia seeds and oats in the almond milk overnight.
- Place the ingredients in a blender and make a smoothie. You can also add ice if you like.

Strawberry Shortcakes

This is a stove top breakfast. It is scrumptious and is an instant hit with children.

Serves 2
Ingredients:

- 1 ¼ cup of whole wheat
- ½ cup of unsweetened coconut
- ¼ teaspoon of baking soda
- 1 tsp baking powder
- ¼ teaspoon allspice
- ¼ teaspoon of nutmeg
- ¼ teaspoon of ground cinnamon
- A pinch of kosher salt
- ½ teaspoon of maple syrup
- ¾ cup of warm water
- ¾ cup of coconut milk
- Oil as required
- Soft serve: Puree of 3 strawberries and 1 banana

Directions:

- Whisk all the dry in dry ingredients and wet ingredients in two separate bowls, making sure that there are no clumps in the wet ingredient mixture. Then mix them together to make the batter.
- Preheat your oven to 250 F in the meanwhile.

- Heat a skillet and pour in some oil. Pour ¼ cup of the batter and make your pancakes. Cook till there are small bubbles on the surface. The bottom should be golden. Transfer them on to a baking sheet and place in the oven.
- Slice 20 strawberries. Serve, the pancakes with the soft serve, strawberries and the maple syrup.

Overnight Parfait

This recipe will definitely make breakfast your favorite meal of the day. You can prepare this and store in the refrigerator overnight.

Serves 1
Ingredients:

- 1/3 cup of regular oats
- 1 tbsp. of chia seeds
- 1 ½ tbsp. of any flavored protein powder
- 1 cup soy milk
- Maple syrup
- Bananas
- Fruits of your choice

Directions:

- In a medium sized pot, bring the soy milk to a slight boil and add the oats, chia seeds and maple syrup.
- Blend the bananas in a food processor to make a soft serve.
- Layer the soft serve, oats and fruits in a tall glass and serve to make a parfait.

Cake Batter Smoothie

Cake batter is the perfect breakfast option. But, to give it a healthy twist, a smoothie twist does the trick.

Serves 1
Ingredients:

- 1 cup almond milk
- 1/3 cup oats
- 1 banana
- 1 teaspoon vanilla
- 1 teaspoon cinnamon
- 1 teaspoon cocoa powder
- 1 teaspoon sweetener
- 1 tbsp. butter
- 1 tbsp. chocolate chips
- Ice cubes

Directions:

- Let the mixed almond milk and oats be mixed together and placed in the fridge to let them soak for an hour.
- Place this in a blender and make a smooth paste. Now add the chocolate chips and pulse till it gets a nice texture.
- Serve cold.

Classic oats

This is a very comfortable breakfast option. Nothing fancy but just simply satisfying. The chia seeds add a great crunch.

Ingredients:

- 1/3 cup of regular oats
- 1 tbsp. chia seeds
- 1 cup almond milk
- 1 ripe banana
- ¼ teaspoon vanilla extract

Directions:

- Mix all the ingredients together and place overnight in the fridge in order to soak.
- Serve the next morning with nuts, blueberries, fruits or any other topping of your choice.

Steel Cut Oatmeal

This is a nutritious breakfast option. The best part is that it makes a great store and serves as breakfast options for those who cannot cook be bothered to cook breakfast every day.

Ingredients:

- 2 cups of water
- 1 cup of steel cut oats
- 2 cups of almond oil
- 2 teaspoon of ground cinnamon
- 2 large, mashed bananas
- 1 tablespoon ground flax and chia seeds
- 2 to 3 teaspoon of vanilla extract
- A pinch of salt

Directions:

- In a medium sized pot bring the water and almond oil to a boil and add the steel cut oats along with a pinch of salt.
- Add the mashed banana, chia seeds and flax. Stir every 5 minutes to prevent lumps.
- Remove from heat when the oats are creamy. Stir in the cinnamon and vanilla extract and serve.

Tips: Add more milk when you serve if you are refrigerating this dish as it may get thick on storing.

Summer Granola

This oil free granola is for those who love a healthy beginning every morning. If you work out in the morning, this serves as a great pre workout snack.

Ingredients:

Wet:
- 2 tablespoon applesauce
- ¼ cup brown rice syrup
- 2 tablespoon of any nut butter of your choice
- 1 teaspoon vanilla extract
- 2 scraped vanilla beans
- ½ teaspoon almond extract

Dry:

- 2 cups of rolled oats
- ½ cup chopped almonds
- ½ cup uncooked millet
- 2 tablespoon ground flax
- 1 tablespoon chia seeds
- ¼ cup brown sugar
- ½ teaspoon Kosher salt
- ½ teaspoon cinnamon

Directions:

- Preheat the oven to 325F and line a baking sheet with a nonstick mat.
- In a bowl, toss the dry ingredients together and separately toss all the wet ingredients except vanilla and almond extracts.
- Microwave this for about 60 seconds and mix it with the wet ingredients.
- Blend the wet and dry ingredients together and stir the whole mixture well till it all comes together.
- Add salt to taste and scoop the mixture onto the baking sheet.
- Bake for about 25 minutes stirring once in between.
- Allow it to cool and then serve. You can even store it in an airtight container.

Quinoa Cakes

Either a savory breakfast option or a super snack time option. Either way it is wholesome and nutritious and enjoyable.

Ingredients:

- 1 ½ cup cooked red or white quinoa
- 2 tablespoons of powdered flax mixed with 6 tablespoons of water
- 1 cup kale, finely chopped with stem removed
- ½ cup ground rolled oats
- ½ cup grated sweet potato
- 2 tablespoons finely chopped onions
- 1 clove of minced garlic
- ¼ cup sunflower seeds
- ¼ cup finely chopped sun dried tomatoes
- ¼ cup finely chopped basil leaves
- 1 ½ teaspoons of dried oregano
- 1 tablespoon of tahini paste
- 1 ½ teaspoon of white wine vinegar
- ½ teaspoon of sea salt
- 3 tablespoons of all-purpose flour

Directions:

- Combine all the ingredients in a large bowl. Stir well till they are mixed well together. Use the flour to bind the ingredients.
- Preheat the oven to 400 F and line a large baking sheet with either cooking spray or a nonstick paper.

- Make patties using this batter and bake them in the oven for about 15-20 minutes or until golden brown. Flip over when one side is done before proceeding to the next.
- Let them cool for a bit before serving.

Vegetarian Baked Dish

Perfect for a Sunday breakfast! Also makes for super snacking option in between meals.

Serves 12
Ingredients:

- 2-3 tbsp. olive oil
- 2 cups chopped onion
- 3-4 garlic cloves, minced
- ½ pound soya chunks, crumbled
- 1 ½ cup diced bell peppers
- 6 cups white or brown bread, cubed
- 1 tbsp. Dijon mustard
- 12 eggs
- 1 ½ cups grated cheese
- 2 cups milk
- Salt and pepper, to taste

Directions:

- Heat a large skillet with olive oil and add the soya chunks till they crumble and are slightly browned. Then add the garlic and onion followed by the bell peppers until softened.
- Now spray a baking dish with cooking spray and layer the bread pieces at the bottom. Follow it up with a layer of the soya chunks.
- Brush it with Dijon mustard and then grate a good layer of cheese over it.

- In a separate bowl, whisk eggs, salt, pepper and milk and pour over the cheese layer and put it in the preheated oven for about an hour, or until the center is set.

Healthy Whole Wheat Pancakes

Everybody loves pancakes! But this one is a healthy version, made of whole wheat!
Enjoy without guilt!

Serves 4-5
Ingredients:

- 1 cup, whole wheat flour
- 1 tsp. salt
- 2/3 cup all-purpose flour
- 1 ½ tsp. baking powder
- ½ tsp. baking soda
- 6 tbsp. butter
- 2 1//2 cups buttermilk
- 2 eggs, beaten to a fluff
- 2 tbsp. brown sugar
- 3 tbsp. unsalted butter

Directions:

- Combine whole wheat flour, all-purpose flour, baking powder, brown sugar, salt and baking soda in a food processor.
- Cut the 3 tbsp. of butter into cubes and mix it with your fingers into the same batter. It should feel and resemble actual sand.
- In this mixture, make a hole in the center and add buttermilk and the beaten eggs and stir till a good mixture is achieved.

- On a hot frying pan, throw in a dollop of butter and ladle out the mixture to make about 4-5 pancakes. Flip them over when bubbles are seen on the first surface. Cook each side for about 2 minutes.
- Serve with maple syrup or your favorite sauce.

Oven Roasted Potatoes

These simple roasted potatoes taste good as a wholesome meal! Serves great as breakfast or as a side dish!

Serves 4
Ingredients:

- 4 tbsp. butter
- Salt and pepper to taste
- 2-3 tsp. fresh rosemary
- 2-3 cloves garlic, minced fine
- 1 ½ pounds potatoes, diced into cubes

Directions:

- Heat an oven prior to preparing for the dish to 450 degrees F.
- Melt butter in a pan and add rosemary, garlic, salt and pepper and add the diced potatoes.
- Transfer the skillet (if it is ovenproof) to the preheated oven, and bake for about half an hour or until golden brown.

- *Tip:* For a yummier version, you can even sprinkle some cheddar cheese on top!

Green Banana Smoothie

Smoothies have always been the healthy breakfast option. Here's a smoothie that is healthy, sweet as well as filling.

Serves 1
Ingredients:

- 1 large banana
- ½ cup soy milk or regular milk
- 2 cups kale, chopped
- 1 tbsp. flax seeds or chia seeds
- 1-2 tsp. honey, depending on desired sweetness

Directions:

- Mash the banana with your hand and add it to your blender, followed by the soy mlk, honey, seeds of your choice and blend at a high speed.
- In your second round of blending, add the chopped kale, and again give it another good blend. Serve this over ice cubes.

Tip: Remember to add the greens to your blender last. This way, it will give you the desired green colour yet not get overtly blended into the smoothie. This also retains the nutrients of the greens a lot longer.

Pita Pockets

This protein rich dish is a great option when you are having a number of people over for a breakfast buffet at home. Easy, filling and a healthy breakfast option.

Serves 1
Ingredients:

- 1 whole wheat pita pocket
- ¼ cup of hummus mixed with any leftover grains or beans.
- ½ sliced avocado
- Slices of iceberg lettuce
- Roasted slices of pepper
- Salt and pepper to taste

Directions:

- Mix the beans, grains and hummus along with adequate salt and pepper in a bowl.
- Line the pita pockets with hummus. Spread this hummus inside the pita halves.
- Finish by layering it with slices of avocado and red pepper.
- You can even grill the pita pocket, if need be.

Pesto Sandwiches

Sandwiches are the yummiest and most filling options for breakfast. Fill it up with any item you desire and butter it, and they will have to taste good!

Serves 2
Ingredients:

- 1 can pesto sauce, store bought or home made
- 1 zucchini, sliced
- 1 onion, sliced
- 1 packet of brown bread
- Butter
- 6-8 button mushrooms, sliced
- 1 small broccoli, cut into small florets
- Handful of olives

Directions:

- Butter the bread slices with a little butter and follow it up with a good coating of pesto sauce.
- Add the sliced zucchini, onions and the lightly sautéed mushrooms and broccoli. Add a sprinkling of olives on top and place it on the grill, buttering the top and bottom.
- Remove when slightly golden on top and serve hot.

Chickpea Pancakes

A change from your regular breakfast options, this high protein breakfast will be good for you. It will most definitely contribute to your protein intake.

Serves 3
Ingredients:

- ¼ cup finely chopped red pepper
- 1 finely chopped green onion
- ½ cup chickpea flour
- ¼ teaspoon sea salt
- Ground pepper as required
- ¼ teaspoon garlic powder
- A pinch of red chilli flakes
- ¼ teaspoon baking powder
- ½ cup and 2 tablespoons of water

Directions:

- Whisk together garlic powder, salt, pepper, chickpea flour, baking powder and red chilli flakes.
- To this, add water and whisk well to get your desired consistency in order to let it resemble a bubbly batter.
- Now add the chopped vegetables to this mixture.
- Heat a skillet and grease with olive oil or cooking spray. Ladle the batter into small or big circles in order to make a pancake.
- Flip over hen one side begins to get small bubbles. Do the same with the other side.
- Serve with your favorite toppings!

Black Bean and Quinoa Salad

Quinoa is something so versatile that it can be had for breakfast, lunch and dinner. A complete protein packed and fiber filled breakfast recipe that will take you through the day comfortably.

Serves 1-2
Ingredients:

For the dressing:

- 2 tablespoons of extra virgin olive oil
- 3 tablespoons of lime juice
- 1 large clove of garlic, minced
- 1 teaspoon of ground cumin
- ½ teaspoon of salt
- 1 teaspoon of maple syrup

For the salad:

- 1 cup of uncooked quinoa
- 1 can of rinsed and drained black beans
- 3 julienned carrots
- 4 chopped green onions
- 1 ½ cup of finely chopped cilantro
- Fine grain salt

Directions:

- In a large bowl toss the quinoa, black beans, cilantro, carrots and green onions.
- Rinse the quinoa and add in a pot with water. Bring to boil and cover with a tight lid. Let it be on simmer for about 20 minutes until quinoa appears light and fluffy. Chill in the fridge for 15 minutes.
- Whisk the ingredients of the dressing together in a small bowl. This dressing can even be prepared a day in advance and kept in the fridge.
- Pour over the salad and toss and add the desired salt and pepper.

Mexican Taco Layered Salad

This makes for a perfect brunch or late breakfast recipe. It also packs well for taking to work as breakfast.

Serves 1-2
Ingredients:

For the macadamia cream:

- 1 cup of macadamia
- 2 tablespoon of fresh lemon juice
- Fine grain salt
- 10-12 tablespoons of water

For the 3 minute-Instant Guacamole

- 1 large avocado
- ¼ cup of chopped red onion
- ½ small, chopped tomato
- 1 tablespoon fresh lime juice
- ¼ teaspoon fine grain salt
- ½ teaspoon ground cumin

For the taco:

- ½ cup soaked walnuts
- 1 ½ teaspoon chili powder
- ½ teaspoon cumin powder
- Freshly ground pepper
- Sea salt

Other ingredients:

- Greens that you like
- Green onion
- Salsa
- Crackers

Directions:

- For your taco: In a food processor blend all the taco ingredients, leaving the walnuts chunky. Place aside in a bowl.
- For the cream sauce: Place nuts in a food processor and add water and lemon juice. You may add more water if needed. Remember to make it a grain-free sauce adding the salt as required upon completing the blending process.
- For the instant guacamole: use the pulp if the avocado flesh as the base and fold the rest of the ingredients in.
- Now for the final dish. Cover the base of a bowl with your preferred greens.
- Add a large dollop of the guacamole followed by the salsa followed by the taco preparations.
- Throw in a generous amount of cream sauce and garnish it with chopped onions and tomatoes.

Black Bean and Hummus Sandwich

This recipe works well for both a salad and a sandwich. Nutritious and satisfying, this recipe can be served for breakfast in the form of a sandwich and for dinner in the form of a salad!

Serves 2
Ingredients:

- 1 seeded and chopped bell pepper
- 4 ounces of sliced mushrooms
- 1 chopped onion
- 8 ounces of roasted bell pepper hummus
- ½ can of rinsed and drained corn
- ½ can of rinsed and drained black beans
- 2 large wheat wraps
- 1 roasted and chopped poblano pepper
- ½ package of fresh spinach, chopped roughly

Directions:

- In a a large skillet, sauté the onions, bell peppers, mushrooms and corn.
- Preheat the oven to about 450 degrees
- Now take your whole wheat wrap and add a layer of hummus onto it followed by the sautéed vegetables with beans, poblano peppers and spinach. Roll into a tight wrap. You can insert a toothpick to hold it still.
- Now place these rolls on a baking sheet and bake for about 10-15 minutes or until slightly brown on the top. Serve warm with a side of salsa and a dollop of sour cream!

Grandma's Granola

This recipe calls for a little patience and lots of care, just like any grandmother does! Breakfast recipes are incomplete without a granola one!

Serves 1
Ingredients:

Wet:
- ¾ cup non-fat vanilla yoghurt
- ½ cup fresh raspberries
- ½ cup rolled oats, the old-fashioned ones!
- 1 tbsp. chopped and toasted almonds

Directions:

- Mix together the oats and yoghurt and store overnight in the refrigerator.
- The next morning, when you remove it to mix in the raspberries and almonds, you would have noticed the oats to have been considerably softer in consistency.
- Serve with a dash of cinnamon.

Chapter 3: Five Bonus Recipes

You can never have enough of breakfast recipes at hand! After going through the previous chapters, here are five bonus Indian breakfast recipes for you! Let's look at how the region of India eats its breakfast and what is so different!

Quick Aloo Parathas

This is one of North India's most famous breakfast recipes. Lip smacking and fulfilling for a hungry soul!

Serves 4
Ingredients:

For the dough
- 1 cup water
- 250g whole wheat flour
- 50 ml oil
- Pinch of salt, for taste

For the filling
- Handful of coriander leaves, chopped
- 500g potatoes, boiled
- 2-3 tbsp. ginger garlic paste
- 1/3 cup onions, diced
- 1 tp. Turmeric powder
- 1 tsp. chili powder
- 1-2 tbsp. lime juice
- Oil, for frying

Directions:

- First boil the potatoes until soft and de-skin them and mash, and keep aside.
- Now finely chop the onions, green chilies and coriander leaves and add it to the boiled potato mixture, along with the rest of the ingredients. To this, add the dough mixture and knead it till it becomes dough that can be rolled into parathas.

- Now to make the parathas. Take each ball of dough and flatten on your palm and roll it flat till it is a small circle.
- Take the rolling pin and roll it out into the form of a tortilla, rounded and smooth.
- Grease and heat a pan on a medium flame with oil and place the rounded parathas on it, one by one, cooking each side till small brown spots appear.
- They will appear golden and cooked through.
- Serve with a spicy pickle or a bowl of curds.

Bread Poha

This is another one of India's most famous breakfast recipes. This recipe always comes in handy when you have leftover bread in the house.

Serves 4
Ingredients:

- 5-6 cup bread, preferably a day old, cubed
- 1 cup fresh or frozen peas
- 1 cup onions
- 3-4 tbsp. oil
- ½ tsp. asafetida powder
- 2 tsp. mustard seeds
- 2-3 whole red chillies
- ½ tsp. chilli powder
- ½ tsp. turmeric
- 2 tsp. salt
- 1/3 cup Lime juice
- ½ cup water
- 1 tsp. green chili paste
- Handful of coriander leaves, chopped

Directions:

- Heat oil in a large pan and add asafetida powder, mustard seeds, curry leaves and whole red chillies, broken into pieces.
- Once it starts spluttering, add the turmeric powder, chili powder, salt, green chilli paste and stir around.
- Add the onions and fry in this mixture till golden brown.

- Soon after add the chopped bread pieces and mix until the masala covers the bread pieces. If you think that the preparation is getting too dry, add a splattering of water.
- Cover for a while and let it cook.
- Remove the lid after about ten minutes and give it a good mixing. Turn off the heat and add lime juice to the mixture and mix it up yet again.
- Serve with a sprinkling of chopped coriander on top.

Uttapam

This is one of South India's most famous breakfast recipes. This recipe always comes in handy when you want a change from your regular dosa preparations but it needs a good amount of preparation time.

Serves 4
Ingredients:

- 2 cups parboiled rice
- ½ cup split urad dal, or Bengal Gram
- 1 cup onions, finely chopped
- 1 cup tomatoes, finely chopped
- Green chillies, finely chopped
- 2 tsp. salt
- ½ tsp. fenugreek seeds
- Handful of coriander leaves, chopped

Directions:

- Soak the dal with the rice and fenugreek seeds the night before. This mixture needs about 5-6 hours' worth of soaking.
- The next morning, grind it to a fine paste, adding salt and water to the mixture, to make it a dropping consistency. This mixture is now to be left outside in order to ferment, for about another 6 hours.
- When the mixture is ready, heat a tawa and pour ½ to 1 cup of batter on it and spread with the back of the spoon.
- Sprinkle the onions and tomato mixture along with chopped coriander on top of it, and cover the uttapam with a lid to let it cook.

- Do not turn over. You will know when the sides start to burn a little and the color of the uttapam changes that it is cooked and can be served.

Steamed Dhokla

This is one of West India's most famous breakfast recipes. This recipe is super healthy as it is steamed and can be made in just a couple of minutes!

Serves 2
Ingredients:

- 1 tbsp. citric acid
- 1 cup besan (Gram Flour)
- 1 tbsp. sugar
- Salt, to taste
- Water
- Pinch of turmeric
- 1 tbsp. baking powder
- Handful of coriander leaves, chopped

For the tadka
- 2 tbsp. oil
- 1 tsp. mustard seeds
- 1 red chilli, broken into small pieces
- 8-10 curry leaves
- Pinch of asafetida

Directions:

- Take a bowl and add the gram flour, salt, sugar, citric acid and a pinch of turmeric. Add water to make it medium thick in consistency.
- Separately, add the baking powder to a glass of water and pour it into the dhokla mixture so that it blends well.

- Now, brush two steaming tins with oil and pour the dhokla batter into it. Steam it in a pressure cooker for about 15 to 20 minutes or until cooked though.
- Remove from the cooker when done and keep aside.
- Now for the tadka! Take a pan and add the 2-3 tsp. of oil. When hot, add the mustard seeds, pinch of asafetida, curry leaves and red chilies. Turn off when it splutters and pour immediately over the steamed dhokla.
- Cut them into pieces and serve it with a smattering of chopped coriander.

Potato and Onion Poha

This is yet another one of Western India's most famous breakfast recipes. Quick to make, and healthy to eat!

Serves 1-2
Ingredients:

- 2 cups beaten or flattened rice
- ½ cup split urad dal, or Bengal Gram
- 1 cup onions, finely chopped
- 1 cup potatoes, diced into cubes,
- 1 tsp. green chilies, finely chopped
- Pinch of asafetida
- 2 tsp. salt
- ½ tsp. mustard seeds
- 8-10 curry leaves
- 2-3 whole red chillies, broken into halves
- ½ tsp. turmeric powder
- 1 tbsp. lemon juice
- Handful of coriander leaves, chopped
- Oil

Directions:

- Wash the beaten rice in a colander, without letting it soak for too long in it. now drain out all the water completely.
- Heat a pan with oil and when hot add mustard seeds, curry leaves, asafetida, and whole red chilies. When it splutters, add the onions and green chilli paste.
- Now add the turmeric powder and put in the potatoes. Fry till they are cooked.

- When the potatoes are nearly done cooking, add the poha, salt and mix till combined well. Cover and cook for a while till potatoes are fully cooked.
- Turn off the heat and add the lime juice and mix well.
- Transfer to a clean dish and serve with chopped coriander.

Conclusion

This book is aimed at helping new vegetarians find inspiration and stick onto the diet, and for old vegetarians to find a way to break out of their monotony of regular meals.

While breakfast is said to be one of the most important meals of the day, people are often at loss as to what to make. Since it is also the first meal of the day, there isn't much time to prepare for it unless you wake up on time. A lot of these recipes take that into consideration, allowing you to make some part of it, the night before.

I hope this book was able to help you find enough recipes to continue your practice of vegetarianism. If you are able to sustain and be motivated towards this noble practice, I will consider the purpose of the purpose of this book to be fulfilled. I do hope that you have a lot of fun in the process of making and creating these recipes too!

Thank you again, for buying this book! I hope it was a pleasure reading it and practicing its recipes!

If you liked *Vegetarian Breakfast Cookbook* you may also like my other books. Check out my Amazon's author page: http://amzn.to/1BqcnEE

Good luck,

Linda Parker

Made in the USA
Middletown, DE
09 January 2018